Purple Ice Cream

Sunni E. Potach

To David - who has been an endless inspiration in my life!

Contents

Introduction

I cannot pinpoint when I began writing poetry. I think I've been poetry for as long as I could write. It has always been an outlet for me- a way for me to express my emotions when I couldn't say it out loud.

For many years, I didn't tell anyone that I wrote poetry. It stayed hidden in notebooks and drawers until my senior year of high school when a Literature teacher used some of my poems for a class. She had asked us to write a poem for class. When I turned mine in, I was called back to her desk and she simply said, "This isn't your first poem." She asked to see others, then used many in class to teach our poetry unit. As an adult, I continued to write but kept them mostly for myself.

Fifteen years ago, my husband encouraged me to compile my poems into a book called *Purple Ice Cream*. The original independent publisher of *Purple Ice Cream* has changed their publishing process and it is no longer available on their site. So I decided to republish it for those who didn't get a copy the first time. Here are the original 17 poems in *Purple Ice Cream*.

Lost Dreams

The dance lessons
   you took for years-
The nights you practiced
until you couldn't walk.

The gymnastic lessons
you took since the day you could stand-
You were going to be the best
through the broken bones and blisters.

The piano lessons
you started in grade school-
You loved Bach, Mozart was too perfect
but Carnegie Hall was waiting.

The life lessons
you began when you were born
don't help when you've fallen apart
the way you do when you've lost dreams.

Your Hands

I sit alone
    in a room
full of strangers
by myself
on the floor
my broken heart
bleeding
in your hands
so strong
yet so fragile
are the hands
that break
love

Her Ocean

She can feel the cold water
flowing over her body
the touch of his hand
was the break
in the waves
that brought her down
to a place only she knew
once in a childhood dream
the eyes of innocence
and thoughts of sand castles
along the shore line
she found the tides
of the sea
somewhere in him
and within herself

she found the endless

emotions of the ocean

as they came together

as though they were meant to be

or had always been one-

his tides

in her ocean

Somewhere In Me

Somewhere in my chest,
there is a big hole
where my heart used to be.

Somewhere in my chest,
there is a lost soul
who cannot see.

Somewhere in my chest,
there is a stain
where you used to be.

Somewhere in my chest,
beneath all that pain
is me.

Darkness

L ife
     falls
across my heart
like dark shadows
in the early morning hours
dancing alone, with itself

Circle That Binds

The circle that binds
lost souls to the world,
the way we always
give in.

The way we love
in the name of hatred,
the way we always
forgive.

The way the world spins
with an angel on its shoulder,
the way we always
give up.

Map

I was blind before I looked into your eyes,
numb before I felt your touch,
and lost until I found
the map to your soul.

Longing

A cold north wind
     joined the southern breeze
as Pele's spirit reigned
inside.

The sky came down
to meet the earth
as I stood by the sea
alone.

In that moment
I said good-bye to the old world
as you said good-bye
forever.

Crash

It's so strange
how we push people away from us-
our very depths
but mainly our hearts.

Human touch
is something that's become rare-
physical affection pushed away
and "wrong" by today's standards.

It's unheard of
to wrap your arms around someone
unless they are deeply hurting-
but why must it be that way?

Why can't we wrap around
the warmth of a good friend?
Or embrace another soul
just having a long, hard day?

Is it really so bad?
Is it physical abuse?
Or are we just afraid of personal affection?
Of what we might *feel*?

I believe that you cannot give a hug
without getting a hug in return.
But what's the worst that could happen-
you get pushed away?

At least you tried-
tried to reach out beyond your power
to another heart
in need of something it doesn't even realize.

And if not, maybe that's why we crash-
we collide into each other in a split second.
We don't realize how much we need each other

until in an instant, we crash.

Another Time and Place

The cold dew
of Sunday morning
runs off the wood deck
and the chair she sleeps in.
remains of the night before
creep up to her again
and remind her of
another time and place.
where flowers grew all year
and children only knew laughter
angels flew with music under their wings
and dreams were only sweet.
there was a gentle embrace
and the soft flow of a long dress
where the only color was love

and the only word was friend.
she opens her eyes
to a new world
beyond her nights
and above her dreams.
the sun that surrounds her
leaves a warm feeling inside
and she remembers that just last night
was another time and place.

Drowning

She looked up at me
green eyes desperate.
She held on
as I tried to stop it.
There was no way to her,
no way to save her.
It had gone too far,
life had gone too far.
Her hand slipped
away from mine,
as she disappeared
into a sea of green eyes.

Under Your Skin

Under your skin
  I breathe you in to me,
You play with my soul,
Leave footprints on my heart.
I show you places in me
that you have never seen.
They are oceans away,
but only you have been.
And only you can taste my tears
or feel the shaking of my laughter.
I stand right here waiting so silently
under a sea of bright stars.
It's amazing what you will do
for the man who stole your water.
But you said you needed to go-

you needed to find yourself.
So I let you go
and if you come flying back to me,
then I know that I will always be
under your skin.

Not the First One

So you left me alone
    with my broken heart
after you threw me
on the ground
and sucked the marrow
out of my life.

Congratulations, Little Boy-
you're not the first one.

Before You Were Gone

for Chad

A nd I miss the things
I never said-
the things I never got to say
before you were gone.

And I miss your smile-
the way your eyes lit up
whenever you were happy
before you were gone.

And I miss your laughter-
a reassuring reminder
of your presence
before you were gone.

I Should've Walked Out

A thousand hugs
and a million lies given,
Something I thought was heaven-
I should've walked out.

A deep, dark secret
in a foreign place,
what I wouldn't give to see that face-
I should've walked out.

A bunch of empty promises,
A ton of hope broken,
happiness gone with the turn of a token-
I should've walked out.

Dreams yet to be fulfilled,
futures yet to be seen,
hearts shattered on a floor once clean-
I should've walked out.

A waltz left to be danced,
a dancer without a partner,
the foot falls a little bit harder
when I should've walked out.

Crossroads

At the crossroads
I found you
lost and wandering
through the darkness
with a shoe full of tears,
Baby's breath
on your shirt,
Your broken heart
in your hands.
The world wasn't what it seemed-
you found that out the hard way.
Life has lead you
to the crossroads,
Fate threw me overboard,
left me

searching desperately
for something that was
always here.

Purple Ice Cream

Everybody has gone now
Everyone has left her
Alone in the doorway
With a single rose
the petals already wilting
The purple ice cream
already melting.

And if they'd just look
far enough into her eyes
They could see who she is,
who she wishes to be,
and what shall never be.

But they can't see her

because the rose has wilted
and the purple ice cream
has melted.

She knows what they wanted
Someone else always does it
better than she ever will.
There are a few small repairs
she'd make within herself
but then she wouldn't be
herself.

She wonders why they can't see her-
can't accept her?
Why must the rose wilt
and the purple ice cream melt?

Her only comfort now
is the music in her head
something that stays
no matter who she is
no matter where she goes
or how many people hurt her.

Lost in the bluebells
as the world spins around one last time,
equipped with her best leather-
the brightly dimmed porch light is on.

But the rose still wilts
and the purple ice cream
always melts.

Acknowledgements

First and foremost, thank you to my husband, David, who has always believed in me more than I have myself. He always encourages me to be better and do better than I am. Thank you to Jonah and Brooklyn, who are my reasons for always striving to be the best version of me I can be. Lastly, thank you to all of my family and friends who have supported me in all my adventures over the years.

"There wouldn't be this if there hadn't been you."

About the author

Sunni is a project manager for an online learning company. She lives with her husband, their two kids, their dog Jet, and their tortoise Isha on the North Shore of Boston. She enjoys reading, hanging out at the beach, traveling, and spending time with family and friends.